THE
BARBICAN
Sarah Foot

BOSSINEY BOOKS

First published in 1988 by
Bossiney Books
St Teath, Bodmin, Cornwall.

Typeset and Printed by
Clowes Book Printers
St Columb, Cornwall.

ISBN 0 948158 47 6

Front cover tinted by Maggie
Ginger: A trawler in full sail
leaving the Barbican.

Back Cover: Nancy Astor
canvassing on the Barbican in
the 1935 election.

Acknowledgments

The Author and Publisher would like to thank the following
people for their help and for kindly lending photographs:
Win Scutt and Plymouth City Museum, Ray Bishop, Alice Boyd,
Caroline Brooks, May Brown, Stanley Edgcumbe, Stanley
Goodman, Mr H. Herring, Mr T. E. Hugo, Robert Lenkiewicz,
Eileen Lillicrapp, Violet McGuire, Jack Nash, Irene Rendle,
George Robey, Peggy Rowe and Joan Smith.

The following photographs were supplied by Plymouth City
Museum and Art Gallery: pages 1, 4, 5, 8/9, 10 upper, lower, 12, 13,
17, 18, 20, 21, 23/24, 26, 27 upper, lower, 28 upper, lower,
29 upper, lower, 30 upper, lower, 31 upper, lower, 32, 33,
34 upper, lower, 35, 36, 37, 38, 39, 40, 41, 42, 44, 45 upper, lower,
46 upper, lower, 47 upper, lower, 48, 49 lower, 50, 52,
53 upper, lower, 54 upper, lower, 55 upper, 56, 57, 58, 59,
60 upper, lower, 61 upper, lower, 62 upper, lower, 63, 64, 65,
66 upper, lower, 68, 88/9, 91, 92, 94/5. Front and Back covers.

About the Author and the Book

Sarah Foot lives in a beautiful converted barn at Elmgate, overlooking the River Lynher. Formerly on the staff of *The London Evening News,* Sarah Foot has written on a wide range of Westcountry subjects in recent years for *The Western Morning News* and *The Sunday Independent* and is the editor of *Cornish Scene,* a quarterly devoted to Cornwall and Cornish causes.

This is her eighth title for Bossiney. She made her debut for the Cornish cottage publishers back in 1979, and *Fowey, River & Town,* an enlarged and updated version of that first publication, remains a Bossiney bestseller.

Here in *The Barbican,* her second Devon title, Sarah Foot explores the unique 'village within the city of Plymouth'. Thoughtfully combining words and old photographs, many appearing in book form for the first time, she takes us on a nostalgic tour of 'the historical heart of the city', and interviews Barbican people who feel that they 'belong to an exclusive club'.

She is the natural author for such a book: deep affection and family links with Plymouth. Her grandfather Isaac Foot was a well-known Plymouth solicitor and Lord Mayor – and was brought up on the Barbican. Her son Charles, like her father and uncles, remains a passionate supporter of Plymouth Argyle. Text and highly evocative illustrations remind us of a world that has gone and yet a Barbican that is still 'alive and throbbing with vitality'. A book for all who love this historic fascinating corner of Devon.

The Barbican

At the turn of the century children were expected to devise their own amusements and although they played in the street they were always carefully dressed. Note the boys in plus fours and hats, some with wide collars, and the girls in pinnies and laced boots.

The Barbican is unique: a village within the city of Plymouth.

Here there is living evidence of the industry and ambition over the years in an area which contrasts sharply with the modern brashness of the city centre.

It is the historical heart of the city and although many of its Elizabethan buildings are well restored and have survived the ravages of time, planners and the blitz of the second world war, the area is no museum.

It remains today as it has always been, alive and throbbing with vitality and retains a separate identity with pride. To have lived and worked on the Barbican or to have parentage from that area is to belong to an exclusive club.

The streets leading to Sutton Harbour saw so many different activities, on which the town later grew prosperous. 'Wine, fish and war, in that order, were the three trades that made Sutton Harbour and through the harbour Plymouth,' wrote Crispin Gill, Plymouth's own historian, who lives on the Barbican.

There certainly was wine in the pubs and beer in the breweries and gin in the ancient Plymouth distillery in Southside Street.

The fishing fleet remains today but the time when the handsome sailing trawlers were moored in serried ranks filling the little harbour are just bright memories.

The times of war are hopefully over although in 1988, with its 400th anniversary celebrations of the defeat of the Armada, we are acutely reminded of Sir Francis Drake living amongst his men in these streets waiting in 1588 to meet the Spanish fleet.

The people of the Barbican, over the last five hundred years and more, have grown used to a great deal of coming and going. So many dramatic voyages have begun from the quays by the harbour-side street. Pilgrim Fathers, adventurers, tradesmen and entrepreneurs – have usually been well received and treated with kindness and encouragement.

As I researched this book and spoke to some of the more elderly inhabitants of the Barbican who could tell me stories handed down by their families over the generations, I came to realise that it is the people who have made the place so special.

Two artists capture the magic of the Barbican: G. H. Jenkins and G. W. Cook. Both pictures are in private collections.

BELOW *Sand barges opposite the Barbican around 1900.*

RIGHT *Fishing smacks prepare for sea.*

OVERLEAF *When the sound of the wind in flapping sails, the call of sailors and fishermen from across the water, the crunch of cartwheel on cobblestones and the stench of gutted fish and fresh horse manure were the background smells and noises on the Barbican.*

Hard times are easily remembered but there is a refrain which came from almost every person I spoke to about Barbican days, especially those who had known abject poverty. It goes something like this: 'We were a close community, everyone cared about everyone else. If you had a loaf of bread and your next door neighbour didn't, then you shared it with them.'

Travellers and tradesmen brought colour and variety to the area. 'Seasonal visitors to Sutton Harbour were the French onion sellers in the late '20s and '30s,' Mr George Robey who lived and worked on the Barbican all his life told me. He was employed by the Sutton Harbour Improvement Company at the age of fifteen. 'They came in their grey wooden boats from St Malo, Paimpol and Treguier,' he added. 'Monsieur Kerberou and Monsieur Jacob were two merchants who came yearly and their stores were on Sutton Wharf. There the onions were spread out on the floor to dry and then vended around the town, first on foot and later by bicycles. Their sabots (which we called clogs) and flat wide caps and berets, together with their strange smelling tobacco, lent an exotic touch in those pre-package-holiday days.

'I think the only person who spoke French on the Barbican at that time was Percy Turner, trawler owner and fish salesman, so if any trawler came into the fish market he became their agent.

'Other yearly foreign callers were the Estonian timber vessels who discharged at Baylys Wharf, Coxside. It was a fine sight to see those huge three-masted schooners with their complicated sails and rigging.

The *Baltic* was one such. Sometimes there were women among the crew, unloading the deal battens and boards.'

But foreigners didn't only come as visitors to the Barbican, sometimes they came to stay.

Caroline Brooks told me about her great grandfather Louis Agazzi, an Italian who came to the Barbican last century. 'He arrived in Plymouth with his young Parisian wife and two eldest children. He was also accompanied by several Italian families – fleeing from conscription into Napoleon's army – who all settled on the Barbican.'

Mr Agazzi tried his hand at many occupations to earn a hard living, including roast chestnut vendor, ice cream seller and beer

retailer. Later, Caroline's grandfather, Jack Agazzi, a well-known Barbican character of the time, worked a fish round in central Plymouth. His cart was pulled by an extremely aggressive pony which, she tells me, would gallop down Royal Parade.

Miss Eileen Lillicrapp, who was born and has lived on the Barbican all her life – she is now 75 – told me that her name came from France, with the Huguenot 'Lille'. 'Crapp', a well-known local name, was added later.

The Barbican has seen many famous visitors: Edward I in 1297 and the Black Prince when he returned from Poitiers with King John of France as his prisoner. Catherine of Aragon came when Henry VII had arranged for her to marry his eldest son. She stayed at the Palace Court, a grand house belonging to John Paynter, a rich merchant and five times Mayor of Plymouth.

'Catherine of Aragon slept here.' Two views of Palace Court before it was demolished in 1879. Later a school was built there. This building was owned by John Paynter one of the wealthiest merchants of Plymouth. It was during his heyday that Catherine of Aragon spent a few nights here on her way to meet her prospective husband, the eldest son of Henry VII. When he died she became the first wife of Henry VIII.

Later the large mansion belonged to the Trelawny family and then became a terrible slum let out to as 'many miserable people as could be crowded into its miserable rooms'. In 1880 part of the building was converted and used as a school; the rest was destroyed.

Mrs Violet Maguire, née Storey, had been a school girl at the Palace Court School. She remembers well the schoolmaster assuring his pupils that 'their sins would find them out'. Violet's father died when she was young and her mother was left with six children to bring up on her own. They all lived in one room, often having to change lodgings to find a cheaper rent.

'I remember there was not often enough money to heat the water for baths,' she says. Their diet consisted of tripe and fish, two foods Violet has been unable to face in her adult life. To make a few extra pennies Violet would sing songs on the corner of the street. She recollects 'Jesus loves me, Yes I know' as being the song that brought most pennies from the passers-by. During the second world war her brother, his wife and their baby daughter were all killed when their house in York Street was bombed.

RIGHT *Three members of the Storey family, Ernest Storey on the right was killed in the blitz in Plymouth and Marion Storey on the left was born in Castle Street. Their little brother James Storey sits in the middle. They were three of six children all brought up by their widowed mother.*

This photograph is of Louis Agazzi and his family, and belongs to Caroline Brooks whose grandfather, Jack Agazzi, is the little boy in the centre. It was probably taken at the turn of the century in the cobbled courtyard of their home in Notte Street.

But despite these hardships Violet talks happily of her childhood and repeats the refrain: 'Everybody helped each other, if you didn't have a shilling someone would always lend it to you. It is an attitude that has completely changed today,' she added.

The picture that was woven for me by these people who were willing to talk about their childhood on the Barbican was a strange mixture of hardship and neighbourliness.

It is hard now to realise that there are people living who can remember a time when an imminent birth meant having to have seven shillings and sixpence for the midwife to come and deliver a baby – on the kitchen table if the bedroom was too crowded with other members of the family – as Eileen Lillicrapp told me.

But it is also wonderful to imagine Eileen as a young girl doing her Sunday job. She rowed the minister of the Seamen's Bethel from ship to ship in the harbour so that he could perform a short service for the seamen on each vessel. 'I remember his text was often "Afloat and Ashore".'

The sea called the tune for most of the people on the Barbican. Whatever their occupation most of them served the seafarers or had a vested interest in a seagoing vessel.

Class of the '30s at the Palace Court School. Violet Storey was a pupil there and remembers the names of some children in that class: Eileen Pearson, Kathleen Jackman, Adelaide Gould, Doreen Darlington, Patsy Glynn, Esther Sterling, Audrey Glinn, Ron Mitchell, George Wood, Freddie Hinch, Annie Gully, Sam Gully, Joyce Smith, Mavis Squance, Clara Mannell, Beryl Owen, Joyce Callicott, Betty Rowe, Jack Roseveare, Bill Jay, Lily Hambly, Ernie Dodge and Peggy Crowl. Many of these names have been associated with the Barbican over the years.

'We lived in the Watch House,' Eileen Lillicrapp remembers, 'and when the tide came up I could jump out of my bedroom window to go swimming.'

Less happily she remembers: 'There was a pawn shop in Gibbin Street and most children can remember their mothers pawning their wedding rings. Men used to pawn their Sunday suits on Monday and reclaim them on pay day in time for church on Sunday. If you took a wet suit you had to pay three pence extra for it to be dried. I've seen false teeth and a glass eye in that pawn shop.'

Just as Violet Maguire would sing songs on the corner of the street as a girl to make a few extra pennies, Eileen had her own job. 'We would spend our days up on the steps of the harbour looking after people's boats for them.' Those steps were first built in 1582 to enable fishermen to reach their boats at low tide.

No wonder Eileen talks proudly of her ability to handle a boat. As a youngster she snatched the championship of the Sutton Harbour regatta from a Miss Rowe of Yealm who had held it for fifteen years.

Because of the appalling conditions on the Barbican there is also history of rampant disease. When cholera struck in 1832, 779 people died. Plymouth was named one of the most unhealthy towns in Britain by a Board of Health Inquiry.

Plumbing facilities were non-existent and one central drain in a courtyard was used by several families while it was not unusual for seven people of three generations to be sharing one room.

Beer houses of varying types were opening on every street on the Barbican in the early part of the last century. They were full of youngsters, some as young as ten years old, who were already taking prostitutes younger than themselves.

The Barbican showing the Watch House where Eileen Lillicrapp was brought up. The slate-faced house with portico and arched windows on the left of the picture was destroyed to widen the street. She felt it was completely unnecessary.

My grandfather, whose family came from the Barbican area, often talked of seeing women begging their husbands to come out of the beer houses before they spent all their hard-earned weekly wage on drink. It was for this reason that he signed the pledge of abstinence at an early age and never wavered from the belief that drink was the root of all evil.

But later there were more respectable pubs and several of the people I spoke to had been born in pubs. Joan Smith, née Bennett, told me that she was born in the Crown and Anchor in 1933. It has now been renovated and was re-christened the Sir Francis Chichester after the intrepid sailor had completed his single-handed trip around the world.

The pub was run by her grandparents Jack and Emma Glanville and later when her parents took over the Thistle Park Tavern in Coxside she would row across to the Barbican to visit her relations.

The eldest of five children she says they led a well-ordered life and were never allowed in the bar during opening hours though she

RIGHT *Emma Glanville in 1936, aged 72, with her daughter Annie Bennett and Annie's husband Orlando Eathorne Bennett (better known as Barrie), the well-known organ builder. He holds his daughter Joan Smith who lent this photograph. She was born at the Crown and Anchor which was run by her grandparents Jack and Emma Glanville.*

LEFT *Turks Head Inn, St Andrew's Street, demolished in 1865, one of the many pubs, beer halls, and drinking places in the Barbican – both then and now. It is well to remember that as many buildings of note have been purposefully demolished as were wiped out by the destructive blitz of the last war.*

remembers getting up to mischief and once removing all the stoppers from the beer caskets so that the beer ran awash down the Barbican street.

Her father was a famous organ builder, Orlando (Barrie) Bennett who died when he was 78 and had the reputation of knowing every organ in the Westcountry and many further afield. He had been re-building the St Andrew's Church organ when the church was bombed in the last war. The organ in the old Plymouth Guildhall on which he had also worked suffered the same fate.

The Barbican was the centre for many lucrative business concerns. For a time all the shipping agents and railway companies had their headquarters here. The Parade, so called because the Marines exercised there in the late seventeenth century, was later used for fish auctions. One can only imagine the stench after the fish debris soaked into the mud, for there were no metalled roads at that time.

The oldest printing works in Plymouth was brought to Southside Street by White Stevens, a journalist and writer – sadly now recently closed.

Huge catches were landed from the trawlers straight onto the quay where the men went to work with their sharp knives and axes. One can only guess at the stench there must have been.

The fishing boom of the later part of the nineteenth century meant that over 5,000 tons of fish were being sent away from the Barbican by rail at a value of over £160,000 in one year. At that time the first steam trawlers were to be seen, and they were to change the face of the fishing business. Sail trawling out of Plymouth began to fail. The first locally built steam paddler was named the *Sir Francis Drake* and launched from Hill's Yard at Cattedown in 1823. In those days fishermen were sometimes still going to sea at the age of seventy or eighty. If you lost your job it was described as 'going to the dumps'.

Rivalries were rife in the area and Sutton Harbour Improvement Company laid their cobbles in a different pattern to that of the Plymouth Corporation.

But the ties were stronger than the rivalries and to this day people from Barbican consider themselves somewhat superior to the rest of the city of Plymouth though the indigenous population with a few rare exceptions may soon no longer exist.

Nowadays, when we are used to fish being carted off to factories already frozen, it is hard to imagine fish being gutted and cleaned on the street.

Two shots of sailing trawlers and rowing boats by the Barbican.

It is interesting to think how many men were highly qualified in seamanship skills at this time. The Barbican supplied all the back-up services for a busy shipping fleet with sailmakers, rope factories and shipbuilders while the coopers made barrels in which ships could carry their provisions. There were also woollen mills, glue factories and breweries. There were 170 people at one time employed in rope making alone on the Barbican where long narrow 'walks' or alleys were necessary for spinning or 'laying up' the rope.

ABOVE The Barbican in 1890 in its commercial heyday showing a hotel, the Great Western & Cornwall Railways office and a fish salesman's premises in the background while the quayside is clustered with people and the harbour with sailing trawlers.

BELOW Looking towards the Barbican, a picture taken in the last century showing the trawlers and steam ship tied up alongside.

OVERLEAF *Scrubbing sails laid out on the quayside.*

These four pages of photographs are taken from an old album bequeathed to Plymouth Museum and they show much of the fishing and maritime activity taking place on the Barbican 100 years ago.

Cleaning fish for market. Women and men both partook of this duty although it was mainly women who would salt and pack the fish into barrels. There are some older residents of the Barbican who can still remember their mothers taking part in this arduous and smelly task.

Tom Fry and his wife selling fish from a barrow.

Cutting up dog fish on the quayside.

Trawlers in Cawsand Bay.

One of the most dramatic sights of the Barbican, the hundreds of fishing trawlers that gathered along the quayside during the great fishing boom of the last century.

ABOVE Horses and drays arrive to pick up their cargoes from the fish quay on the Barbican with the sails of the trawlers in the background.

BELOW Fishermen stand around a catch of dog fish. November to February was the high season for dogfish, otherwise known as flake, and as many as 30,000 were sometimes landed in one day in the early 1920s.

ABOVE A tug guides a large trawler into the harbour.

BELOW Early 1900s – a view from the East Pier at Coxside looking at the West Pier with an upturned cannon being used as a bollard.

RIGHT An old house in Notte Street, pictured in 1880. Notte Street
was the home of many successful people including Cookworthy,
the man to make the first porcelain in Britain. Some fine examples
of his work can be seen at the City Museum.

LEFT Whitaker's Smoke House which was started in Victorian times by two Cornish fishermen from Newlyn. Herrings were smoked here and the workforce was made up of over forty people, mainly women. Chickens, cats and dogs roamed the streets collecting the bits cast aside and the smell of smoked fish pervaded the area. Deliveries of fish were made throughout the town by horse and cart.

FAR RIGHT The Pope's Head in Looe Street, a principal inn in Plymouth till Foulston, the architect who transformed Plymouth in the last century, finished the Royal Hotel in 1811.

ABOVE Drake lived at the top of Looe Street. Apprentices lived in tenements at the back of the Merchant's House (now a fine museum) while fishermen and poorer people lived in smaller houses nearer the waterside. There were small courtyards at the back of most of the houses.

RIGHT An elaborately carved wooden door taken from a dwelling in Looe Street and now on show in the City Museum.

Plymouth's Old Workhouse, the site on which Plymouth's
Guildhall now stands. This is in fact beyond the area of the
Barbican but many of those who worked on the Barbican lived
here in this somewhat majestic, though no doubt depressing,
building. You can see the grand tower of St Andrew's Church
behind.

Hoe Gate, the last surviving gate into Plymouth, was demolished
in 1863. It was one of the old town gates giving entry through the
town walls enclosing the old port. It was near to this gate that the
public baths serving the Barbican were situated.

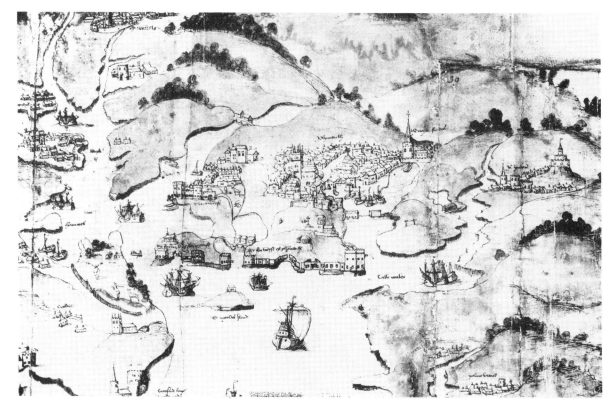

ABOVE A map of Plymouth in the sixteenth century. It is
interesting to note how most of the building took place between
Charles Church and St Andrew's Church and how fortified the
town was at that time forty years before the threat of the Armada.

RIGHT Over two hundred years later, a late eighteenth century
map of Plymouth and the Citadel.

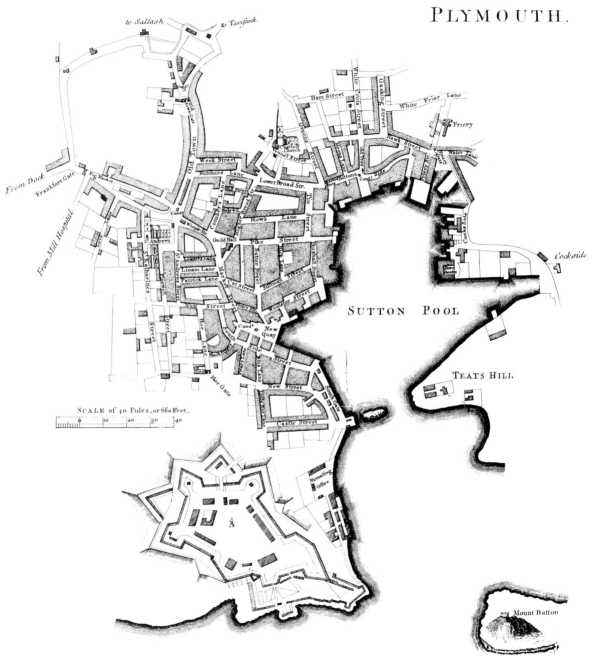

A PLAN
of the
TOWN and CITADEL
of
PLYMOUTH.

to Saltash
to Tavistock

From Dock
Frankfort Gate
From Mill Hospital

White Cross Street
Gasking Street
Ham Street
White Friar Lane
Friery
Charles Church
Tunnel Street
Water Lane
Week Street
Butchers Lane
Lower Broad Str.
Cockside
Cockside

SUTTON POOL

TEATS HILL

SCALE of 40 Poles, or 660 Feet.
0   10   20   30   40

Guild Hall
St Andrews
St Catharines
Linam Lane
Patrick Lane
Mill Street
Hoe Lane
Hoe Gate
New Quay
New Street
Castle Street
South Gate
Victualling Office

Mount Batton

ABOVE The Citadel was built in Plymouth following the civil war. Plymouth supported Cromwell and stood out against the Royalists through years of hardship. When Charles II came to the throne he did not trust the people of Plymouth so he built his Citadel with guns that faced both out to sea and into the town. This view, taken from the Citadel, shows the amount of activity which took place in the Cattewater and Sutton Pool.

Lord Boringdon, from nearby Saltram House, was responsible for laying mooring chains in the Cattewater in the early part of the nineteenth century. By the latter part of that century there were twenty to thirty vessels built each year in Plymouth and there were six ship builders in the Cattewater alone.

RIGHT The Citadel was built in 1666 and the grand Gateway is one of the nation's best examples of baroque architecture. It was built on the site of the former fort for which Drake and Hawkins were responsible.

It is not known why the niche at the top of the elaborate gateway has never been filled. Was it to contain a statue of Charles II?

Some fine pictures of the Plymouth Regatta over 100 years ago. It was a day of enjoyment for all those who had earned their living through often dangerous and arduous duties at sea. When the large old hulks and steamers dressed over-all and the little rowing boats wended their way between them Plymothians were able to indulge in some real enjoyment.

Regatta day was a day that people on the Barbican particularly
enjoyed as many of the visitors to Plymouth for that occasion
would wander through the narrow streets buying the souvenirs
and delicacies sold along the pavements. Festivals in days of
hardship were always celebrated with gusto.

Regatta time in Sutton Harbour was always a great event.
The people in the foreground here were Brazilians, just one of the
many nationalities who visited the Barbican area over the years.

The first Plymouth Regatta was held in 1827. Soon after this the Royal Western Yacht Club was opened and remains one of the highly regarded clubs of its kind in the world.

Mayflower Steps. It was in the year 1620 that the *Mayflower* sailed for America bearing the brave and intrepid passengers who were determined to find a country where they could worship God in their own way. The ship had come into Plymouth for repairs and the crew were 'kindly entertained and courteously used by divers friends'.

Over two hundred years later in 1891 a tablet was placed in memory of this occasion and to commemorate the visit to Plymouth in July of that year of a number of The Pilgrim Fathers' descendants and representatives.

There were many departures made from Plymouth in the nineteenth century. As many as half a million English and Irish emigrants left for the British colonies from Sutton Pool. Prices for journeys that were uncomfortable and dangerous were cheap by today's standards. For as little as half a guinea you could sail from Cork to Plymouth and then onto North America for 8 guineas and Australia for 14 guineas.

BELOW RIGHT A painting by Bernard F. Gribble in Plymouth City Art Gallery of the Departure of the Pilgrim Fathers in 1620.

BELOW The replica of the *Mayflower*, launched in 1957 to repeat that voyage across the Atlantic.

On the 6ᵗʰ of September, 1620, in the Mayoralty of Thomas Fownes after being "kindly entertained and courteously used by divers friends there dwelling," the Pilgrim Fathers sailed from Plymouth in the Mayflower, in the Providence of God to settle in NEW PLYMOUTH, and to lay the Foundation of the NEW ENGLAND STATES ⌒ The ancient Cawsey whence they embarked was destroyed not many Years afterwards, but the Site of their Embarkation is marked by the Stone bearing the name of the MAYFLOWER in the pavement of the adjacent Pier. This Tablet was erected in the Mayoralty of J.T. Bond 1891 to commemorate their Departure and the visit to Plymouth in July of that Year of a number of their Descendants and Representatives.

MAYFLOWER
1620

30 9 13
S.J

A new ornamental structure was placed at the Mayflower steps in 1934, paid for by Sir Frederick Winnicott. Hundreds of tourists flock each year to the monument to remember the Pilgrims who left from this very spot in September 1620, and the names of the Pilgrim fathers are printed on the Island House where some of them stayed.

MAYFLOWER
1620

Elizabethan House, New Street which was built in 1580. The interior of this carefully restored building makes a nostalgic and atmospheric museum. Walk around the rooms and you will soon be aware of the way people lived in the sixteenth-century Barbican. Streets were so narrow you could almost shake hands with the people living opposite and backyards were small and cramped and enclosed.

One is aware that although people grumble about modern noise from traffic and engines there must have been very little chance to enjoy silence in Elizabethan days with the sound of people, animals, carts and the general paraphernalia of over-populated areas in extremely narrow streets.

The furniture displayed in the Elizabethan House has all been carefully chosen to be of the right date and to those of us used to twentieth-century space and comfort it seems most austere though very beautiful.

Carved wooden beds, chairs and chests are well displayed, while the sloping wooden floors and low ceilings with doorways built for dwarfs give a cramped feeling to the building.

This stout lady holding what looks like a Bible was called Sarah Jane Congdon (née Tucker). She was apparently born in the house now known as the Elizabethan House. She was grandmother to May Brown who kindly lent the photograph.

It was in 1930, after an ambitious fund raising enterprise, that the Elizabethan House was opened to the public and remains to this day a museum that uniquely conjures up the past, where one can wander from room to room and imagine the kind of life that was lived when New Street was indeed new in Queen Elizabeth I's reign. Alderman Churchward and Lady Nancy Astor were the main personalities taking part in the opening ceremony, which brought a mixed and interested crowd. Lord and Lady Astor had given a substantial contribution towards the preservation and repair of the fine old building.

Lady Nancy Astor was one of the best-known and best-loved characters of Plymouth. Following in her husband's footsteps as the local Member of Parliament, she claimed fame as the first woman Member of Parliament to take her seat in the House of Commons, after a by-election in 1919.

A colourful and outspoken figure she canvassed in and around the Barbican through the '20s and '30s to great effect. A teetotaller, she was mistrusted by the publicans who sometimes ordered her off the premises but often ended up by voting for her.

Four scenes from Lady Astor's album of the election campaign in December 1935, all on the Barbican.

Lady Astor invited many well-known figures to Plymouth and
after the second world war brought the plight of the bombed city
to the notice of many influential people. Such figures as Charlie
Chaplin and Bernard Shaw came to assist her in her many
projects for Plymouth and were proud to be seen alongside the
direct and forthright woman who gave so much of her time,
energy and resources to the town she loved so well. Here she is
with Charlie Chaplin at a Fishermen's Service on the Barbican in
1931. And, right, at the opening of the Margaret McMillan Day
Nursery.

In 1925 when the social conditions of the Barbican were almost unbearable and Plymouth was one of the most unhealthy towns in Britain, Lord and Lady Astor were determined to help promote social services for the community.

Virginia House Settlement was established in a group of old buildings to encourage education, welfare and good health. For twenty years it played a major role in helping to alleviate the many hardships of the population of the Barbican.

Our picture shows Lady Astor with the gymnasium club at Virginia House in 1935, obviously as popular with the young then as the Keep Fit Class and aerobics are now.

Today the work at Virginia House is being revived and a busy charitable organisation is trying to cater for the different needs of the people of new Plymouth.

One interesting project is being tackled under the Virginia House auspices by a student from Plymouth Polytechnic, Kay Isbell. She is putting together a pictorial and oral history of the Barbican area and has interviewed on tape many people who can tell stories of Barbican life before the 1930s. The recordings will 'unlock the door to the rich and poetic world of oral tradition and vernacular speech, dialect and languages,' she says.

RIGHT Nancy Astor campaigning in Notte Street.

BELOW In July 1962 the Queen walked through the streets of the Barbican after opening the new Civic Centre in Plymouth. This Parliamentarian town was transformed into a Royalist city for the day.

LEFT The opening of the Tinside improvements and swimming baths on the Hoe in 1931 brought a whole new aspect to the life of the people on the Barbican who were able to make the most of these amenities. The picture shows how many people gathered for the ceremony on a June day in 1931.

BELOW The Fish Quay from the Pier Head during Regatta day 1935. In the rowing boat is Walter Lillicrapp in cap. Note sailing trawlers in background.

Children playing round a lamp post with an old Barbican warehouse in the background and the cobbled streets that still exist. Note the sign for carpenter and undertaker, two occupations that traditionally were carried out by the same firm, as with the Foot family who lived on the Barbican in the later part of the nineteenth century. They ran a builder's and undertaker's business there for many years, remaining in Plymouth until Isaac Foot started his own solicitor's firm, named Foot and Bowden, which still exists in North Hill under the same name. Their house and workshop was in Notte Street. The author remembers her grandfather Isaac Foot saying that when they left the Barbican to live in the more salubrious part of Plymouth he missed the close comradeship amongst Barbican neighbours, a sentiment echoed by many of the ex-residents of the area.

RIGHT Isaac Foot Senior, the author's great grandfather, who started his building business in the Barbican.

ABOVE Isaac Foot Senior and his wife Eliza.

69

Nos 24 and 25 The Parade, Barbican. No 25 is pictured round about the turn of the century and was then Cooke's Dairy. This building is now the studio of Robert Lenkiewicz who has become Plymouth's own artist in residence. He has painted several startling murals throughout the town, the best known of which is on the wall face outside his studio. This building and No 24, T. W. Reeby, Fruiterer and Greengrocer both belonged to the Nash family who had a vegetable business on the Barbican for over a hundred years.

Jack and Jim Nash were responsible for the present consortium of shops now in the House that Jack Built. Their great grandfather John Oxley Nash was a gifted water colourist who exhibited at the Royal Academy. He found that potatoes were much cheaper in Scotland than in Plymouth and started his business by transporting them to the town. He kept his boat, the *Ocean Monarch,* moored alongside the Barbican. The Nash business had its own horses and wagons and at one time employed 30 people. The family married into the Foot family who were also closely connected with the Barbican area with their building business in Notte Street. Find a street in Plymouth with a Methodist name and you can be almost certain that it was built by Isaac Foot Senior's firm.

RIGHT Eliza Jane Foot, sister of
Isaac Foot Junior, who married
James Latimer Nash.

LEFT 'The Last Judgment', the world-famous mural by painter
Robert Lenkiewicz, on the Southside Street façade of the House
that Jack Built Craft Arcade. The window containing 4,000 pieces
of glass was made by Adele Nash.

Photographs from the family collection of Eileen Lillicrapp.

LEFT Her father James Lillicrapp.

RIGHT This photograph is rather damaged but it shows Eileen's mother on the far right when she was forewoman during the first world war making ammunition boxes at Coxside.

BELOW Two photographs of day trips for the crew and employees of the Commercial Cable Company in the 1920s. Eileen's brother and brother-in-law worked there.

75

Mrs May Brown has lent these photographs of her family. The old lady in the white bonnet is her great-great-grandmother Tucker who owned her own boats, housed apprentices, knitted their jerseys and sold her own fish. 'I believe she was a tough old bird,' says May Brown.

The gentleman holding the top hat and the lady in the dark crinoline were her other great, great grandparents by the name of Congdon. He was secretary to the Seaman's Bethel for a time.

Two more family photographs show great grandfather Tucker (left) and father Edwin Charles Congdon (right) when he had become a fish salesman.

LEFT An earlier photograph of May Brown's father as a young
fisherman (on the right).

M. READING,

Refreshment House
and Board Lodgings,

Bed and Breakfast   Moderate Charges

SHIPPING SUPPLIED

7 & 8 THE BARBICAN, PLYMOUTH.

General Provisions   Tobacco and Cigarettes

Large and Small Parties Catered for
at Moderate Charges.

Mary Reading, still well remembered by some elderly people living on the Barbican, ran a famous boarding house where fourteen people could stay. Her daughter, Irene Rendle, who was one of five children, says her mother worked too hard for her own good.

The building which housed this remarkable establishment providing sweet shop and grocery store, bed and breakfast and meals, was bombed in the blitz.

Irene Rendle told me that from the age of eleven she worked alongside her mother. 'It was hard work, a lot of scrubbing, but my mother looked after us like Lords and Ladies.' She also says her mother boasted that no-one on the Barbican would go without so long as she could provide. 'Often people would come for a meal and they got it whether the money came back or no,' Irene told me. Mary Reading died at the age of 54 in 1957. 'I reckon she worked too hard and that's why she went so soon,' her daughter told me.

Mrs Jane Hannam who ran Hannam's Cookshop for fishermen for fifty odd years. This is now called Piermasters. Her maiden name was Charlick and she was yet another of the strong female characters who are so well remembered on the Barbican.

Born in 1884 she died in 1970 and is pictured here at 33 Southside Street on the Barbican in front of her old range.

Captain Daymond was in charge of the tugs of Messrs. Reynolds & Co., Torpoint. He was rather deaf, hence the hand behind the ear in this photograph taken in 1935. His son Stanley was also on the tugs that regularly relieved the crews of the Eddystone Lighthouse in all weathers.

James William Waye, the landlord of the United Services pub at
the top of Castle Street, known as No 1 Garrison Green, from the
1880s until just before the 1930s. Here he is with nine of his
eleven children, all of whom were born at the pub. The
photograph belongs to his grandson T. E. Hugo who tells me that
his grandfather as well as being the publican also kept two small
fishing vessels which were known as 'hookers' and kept a parrot
in the pub whose language was atrocious due to the teachings of
the regular customers.

Some photographs from the collection of Mr George Robey.

LEFT Guy's Quay, Woolster Street, in 1935.

RIGHT Sutton Harbour Improvement Company at 29-30 Woolster Street taken in 1935 when Mr George Robey was working there.

ABOVE Interior of the offices of the Sutton Harbour Improvement
Company at 29 Woolster Street, 1935. Up to that date all walls
were painted dark green and were gas lit.

RIGHT Mr Robey at work in
the Cattewater office of the
company in the 1930s.

LEFT Billy Hole in the offices of the Cattewater Harbour
Commissioners, The Exchange, Woolster Street in 1935. First
employed by Jack Balkwell, Harbour Pilot, he later became self
employed and plied to and from the vessels in the Sound.

BELOW Billy Hole (right) and his assistant Walter Lillicrapp in the
motor boat *Dorothy* in 1935. As a youth Billy lived in Island House
just seen in rear. By the Fish Market is the steam trawler
Oakwold.

Some fine characters on the Barbican.
Note the gas light behind the figures.
It was not unusual for men to
continue sea-faring occupations into
their seventies and some even into
their eighties.

The Barbican Group

Stanley Goodman who has fought long and hard in the best interests of the Barbican, and who has been Chairman of the Barbican Group since its inception in 1975, writes about the aims of this conservation society.

The proper title for this consultation group is the 'Conservation Society for the Outstanding Conservation Area of Plymouth Barbican'. The word 'outstanding' is part of the statutory title ... even the London boffinery recognise that Barbican is 'special'.

Even before Conservation Areas were invented, the Barbican had its own 'special care' committee ... formed of one third local councillors, one third Barbican traders and one third the City Council's professional officers. The task was to 'restore' Southside Street to its eighteenth-nineteenth century appearance along the lines of the successful Magdalen Street experiment in Norwich under Duncan Sandys. All modern intrusions were banished ... high wires, lamp posts, modern pillar boxes etc ... together with the 'reform' of things like shop names and lettering. Colour of the

LEFT An oil painting of Stanley Goodman by Robert Lenkiewicz.

RIGHT Pin's Lane looking towards Southside Street. Showing exactly how narrow and congested Barbican streets were in the last century.

Seagulls and sails coming into
harbour . . .

shops and houses was to conform to an eighteenth-century type
scheme worked out by the City Architect. After a few doubts
about cost the scheme was a success and drew increased trade.

Then came 'Conservation' and the need for a guardian society
to see that nothing was spoilt by intrusive modernity or unsuitable
uses. Planning control for change of use and 'development' is
exercised by the City Council's Planning Committee – and they
put all Barbican plans before the Barbican Group prior to going to
committee. They thus obtain a 'grassroots' view which is usually
thought to be helpful in arriving at a generally acceptable plan. In
this way the Barbican residents get to know the details of any
possibly objectionable plan early enough to make their feelings
known (and published) before the Planning Committee's dictate
finally descends on the plan. This is a really useful piece of public
relations . . . it is the sudden unwarned activity next door which
upsets the local citizen. The citizen who feels that he or his
organisation has been consulted is gratified and likely to feel that
he 'is part of things'. The membership of the Barbican Group is
peculiar . . . it includes nobody and everybody. Any Barbican
resident, anybody who has an interest in Barbican is a 'member'
and can (and does) come to the monthly meeting in the
'Boatmen's Shelter' to say his mind.

The Group does other things, of course. They support the Council's effort to repave Southside Street with that lovely Plymouth limestone that looks like veined marble when wet and the careful restoration of the ancient cobbled surfaces of New Street – a surface which is itself 'Listed' because Francis Drake and his contemporaries walked on it.

The Barbican is so small (basically three small streets) that the tide of visitors and coaches is always threatening to strangle it. To get the scurf of parked cars out of Southside Street it needs a carpark close by ... and when the Council proposed to do just that by building a three-decker on the scrag end of the Hoe by Garrison Green, English Heritage was scandalized and got the Department of the Environment to 'call it in'. The Group gave evidence to the Inquiry on 5 July 1988 to support the Council.

RIGHT A G. H. Jenkins watercolour of the Barbican painted in the early part of this century.

Other Bossiney Titles Include

E.V. THOMPSON'S WESTCOUNTRY
This is a memorable journey: combination of colour and black-and-white photography. Bristol to Land's End happens to be the Bossiney region, and this is precisely E.V. Thompson's Westcountry.
'Stunning photographs and fascinating facts make this an ideal book for South West tourists and residents alike — beautifully atmospheric colour shots make browsing through the pages a real delight.'
Jane Leigh, Express & Echo

MYSTERIOUS PLACES
by Peter Underwood
Visits locations that 'seem to have been touched by a magic hand'. The man who has been called Britain's No. 1 ghost hunter reflects: 'We live in a very mysterious world ...'
'... an insight into some of the more mysterious places in the south west.'
David Elvidge
Launceston & Bude Gazette

DARTMOOR IN THE OLD DAYS
by James Mildren
James Mildren is an author who is at home in the wilderness of his Dartmoor.
'Lovers of Dartmoor will need no persuasion to obtain a copy. To anybody else, I suggest they give it a try. It may lead to a better understanding of why many people want Dartmoor to remain a wonderful wilderness.'
Keith Whitford, The Western

MYSTERIES IN THE DEVON LANDSCAPE
by Hilary Wreford & Michael Williams
Outstanding photographs and illuminating text about eerie aspects of Devon. Seen on TSW and Channel 4. Author interviews on Devon Air and BBC Radio Devon.
'... reveals that Devon has more than its share of legends and deep folklore.'
Derek Henderson
North Devon Journal Herald

CASTLES OF DEVON
by James Mildren
The well-known Westcountry journalist tours 16 castles.
'Mr Mildren, whose love for the Westcountry is obvious and contagious, digs out many fascinating nuggets ...'
Western Evening Herald

DARTMOOR PRISON
by Rufus Endle
A vivid portrait of the famous prison on the moor stretching from 1808 — with rare photographs taken inside today.
'The bleak Devon cage's 170 year history ... fascinatingly sketched by one of the Westcountry's best known journalists Rufus Endle ... the man with the key to Dartmoor.'
Western Daily Press

DART — THE MAGICAL RIVER
by Ken Duxbury
Rising high on Dartmoor, the twin rivers, East and West Dart, merge to flow to the sea at Dartmouth.
'The book is a clever blend of history, topography and personalities, all of which combine to create a marvellous image of both the river and its communities.'
Richard Armstrong, Totnes Times

PLYMOUTH IN WAR & PEACE
by Guy Fleming
Bossiney's 150th title by the well-known journalist of the Western Evening Herald. Never has the saying 'every picture tells a story' been more vividly demonstrated. The blitz and Plymouth Argyle, famous politicians and the Navy, the Barbican and the rebirth of the city are only some of the features.

HISTORIC INNS OF DEVON
by Monica Wyatt
The author visits 50 famous hostelries scattered over the county.
'Monica Wyatt's writing is pitched at just the right level ... thoroughly researched, shot through with real enthusiasm and never donnish. She shares her discoveries with you ... I raise my glass.'
The Western Evening Herald

LEGENDS OF DEVON
by Sally Jones
Devon is a mine of folklore and myth. Here is a journey through legendary Devon. Sally Jones brings in to focus some fascinating tales, showing us that the line dividing fact and legend is an intriguing one.
'Sally Jones has trodden the path of legendary Devon well ...'
Tavistock Times

WESTCOUNTRY MYSTERIES
Introduced by Colin Wilson
A team of authors probe mysterious happenings in Somerset, Devon and Cornwall. Drawings and photographs all add to the mysterious content.
'A team of authors have joined forces to re-examine and prove various yarns from the puzzling to the tragic.'
James Belsey, Bristol Evening Post

SUPERNATURAL ADVENTURE
by Michael Williams
Contains a great deal of unpublished material relating to the Supernatural.
'Spiritual healing, automatic writing are just a few of the spectrum of subjects ... neat, well presented ... easy-to-read volume.'
Psychic News

We shall be pleased to send you our catalogue giving full details of our growing list of titles for Devon, Cornwall, Somerset and Dorset as well as forthcoming publications. If you have difficulty in obtaining our titles, write direct to Bossiney Books, Land's End, St Teath, Bodmin, Cornwall.